AUSTRALIA

the gift

Contents

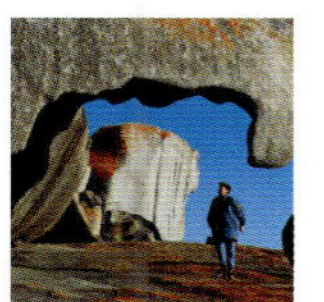# Australia, the Gift

Australia, the island continent, is a country like no other. An ancient land, it is still drifting north slowly, so slowly, from where it lay as part of Gondwana, joined to the landmasses of South America, Africa, Antarctica and India. The fragile Australian environments rest on a skeleton of eroding mountain ranges that drop off in spectacular escarpments, extinct volcanoes, vast plains and deserts, rocky coasts carved by wind and water, golden beaches, and the continental shelf, home to magical coral reefs and cays in the tropics and rocky reefs and kelp forests in the temperate zones.

Long isolated from the life-forms of other lands, the flora and fauna of Australia have developed to be unique – no other place can boast the richness of marsupials and reptiles that are found here. Nowhere else can be found the glorious flowering gums, wattles, banksias and melaleucas that abound in the Australian bush. No-one who has not visited the Outback can imagine just how beautiful it is to see the desert bloom after rain. The birds of Australia grace the land; there are the brilliant hues and joyous shrieks of the rich array of parrots, the proud elegance of the waterbirds, the soaring majesty of the birds of prey, the glints of flashing colour of the fairy-wrens, finches, kingfishers, riflebirds and pittas, the melodious song of the bush birds, and the harsh cries and keen intelligence of the crows and ravens.

Australia holds an extraordinary array of climates and habitats – from the dense beauty of the tropical rainforest to the spare, dramatic, central deserts, from the coastal heathlands to the wetlands of Kakadu, from the forests of mighty eucalypts on the flanks of the ranges to the stunted scrubs of mallee and mulga, from windswept alpine pastures dotted with twisted snow gums to deep, lush valleys where water cascades through ferns – these all form the gift to the world that is Australia, a land of great bounty, and of contrasts and extremes. This land is priceless, and so much of it is still little known.

Granite is wrought into mystic shapes and painted with lichen, like the sculpture of giants, at Remarkable Rocks, Kangaroo Island, South Australia.

Queensland

"Queensland… Beautiful one day, perfect the next!" says the slogan, and that is close to the truth. From unquiet beginnings in 1825 as the Moreton Bay Penal Colony, the European settlement on the banks of the Brisbane River grew and prospered. When the transportation of convicts ceased in the mid-1800s, pioneering free settlers spread further from Brisbane. Queensland was proclaimed a colony in 1859, and, in 1901, became one of the six States in the Commonwealth of Australia.

Many tribes of indigenous people have dwelt throughout Queensland, indeed, throughout Australia, for untold thousands of years. Their history is recorded in the art on the walls of caves and gorges, in the oral traditions of the people, and in the shell middens, fish traps and artefacts of daily life.

Occasionally someone on horseback will catch a glimpse of reflected light in a creek bed or on a rocky slope… There will lie a beautifully worked stone axe, dropped in the haste of the hunt, or lost when the fibre lashings broke and the head fell free from the handle. The finder stares at it, imagining how the owner must have regretted the loss of this laboriously ground and shaped treasure.

Queensland is vast, the second largest State in Australia, and it covers an astonishing range of environments, from the woodland and monsoon forests of Cape York to the rainforests of the Daintree, from the eucalypt forests of the Great Dividing Range to the scrub, grass plains and deserts of the West, from the long golden beaches and stunning sand islands of the coast to the subtropical rainforest and tumbling waterfalls of the Border Ranges. And then there is the glory of the Great Barrier Reef. Perhaps the State's most wondrous sight, the Reef stretches over 2000 kilometres from Torres Strait south down the east coast of Queensland to Bundaberg.

These diverse habitats abound with strange, wonderful plants and animals, and landscapes of staggering beauty and variety. It is here that our experience of the island continent begins.

The deep, rich colours of the rock walls are reflected in the quiet, clear waters of Lawn Hill Gorge. All is wrapped in the lush green of a slip of cabbage palm, fig and pandanus forest isolated from the surrounding arid plains when climate change came and dried the inland.

LAMINGTON NATIONAL PARK

Cool and misty, Chalahn (opposite), Elabana and Coomera Falls, leap down cliffs, plunging into deep pools.
Lichen-encrusted giants reach upward to the light in the primeval mountain rainforests of the Border Ranges.
Animals and birds – the Short-eared Possum (opposite, top left), Regent Bowerbird (opposite, centre left), and
Black-striped Wallaby (opposite, bottom left) – live safe from the ways of humans in this soft, dimly lit haven.

THE BUNYA MOUNTAINS

The fruit of mighty pines with spreading, up-turned branches radiating from the massive trunks, fed a multitude
when the Aborigines gathered for ceremonies and feasts. Rare grasses thrive there now, carpeting the "balds",
which are the high altitude grasslands.

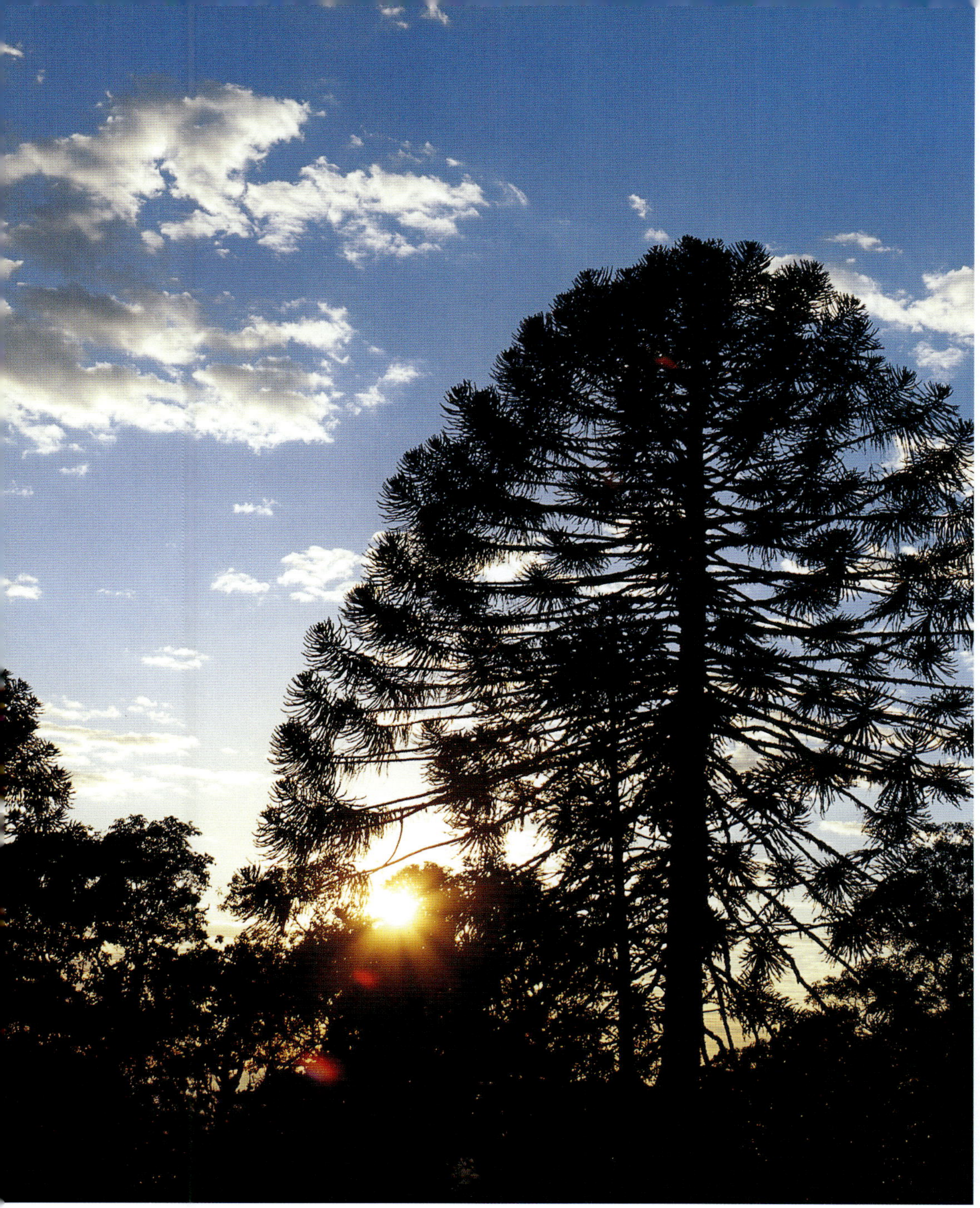

ON THE MAIN LINE OF THE GREAT DIVIDING RANGE

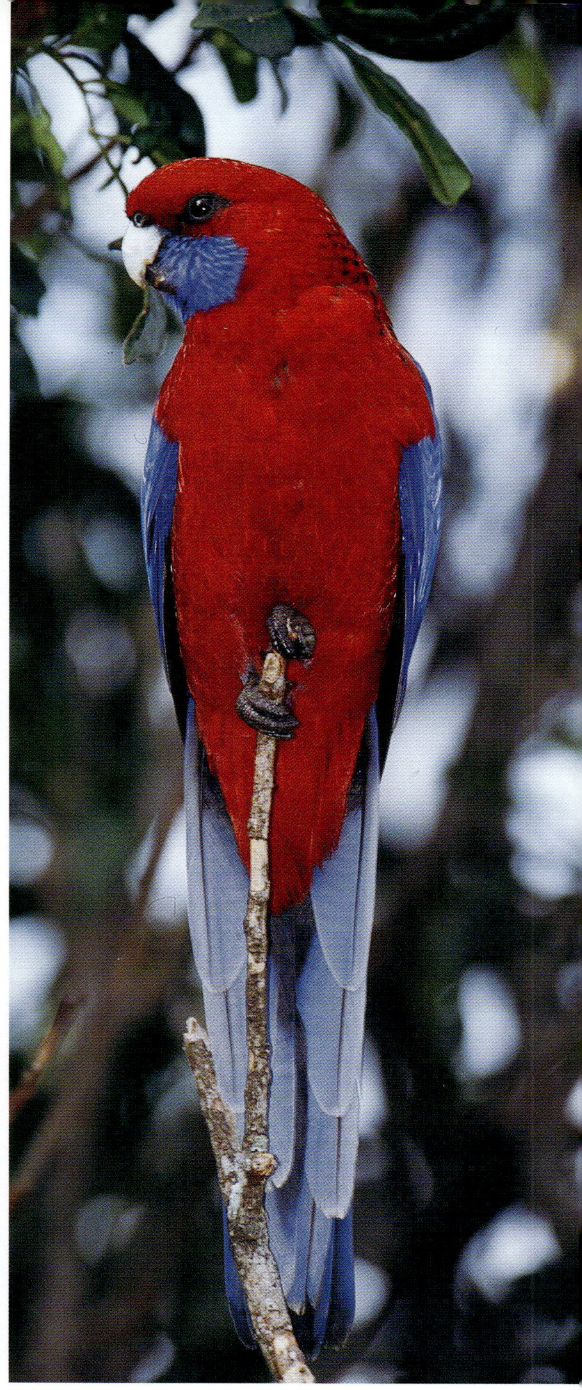

The animals, such as the Red-necked Pademelon, shelter in the pines and tall gums, the trees and logs covering and protecting them between ventures onto the grasslands. Bright wings shimmer in shafts of sunlight as Crimson Rosellas flit from branch to ground to bush to treetop.

THE GREAT BARRIER REEF

Deep peacock blue, aquamarine, green like oiled silk, pale clear blue, sweeps of golden sand, leaf-green, dark
mottling where the coral lies – these are the colours of the islands, reefs and cays when seen from plane or boat.
Lady Musgrave Island's lagoon and fringing reef exemplify the World-Heritage-Listed reef's riches.

RIBBON OF LIFE

Below the surface, the palette changes in the twinkling of an eye – scales flash silver and a multitude of hues.
This delicately balanced ecosystem that has formed over thousands of years teems with animal and plant life of
astonishing variety – more than two million species are named and there may be as many yet to be identified.

THE WHITSUNDAY ISLANDS

Emerald islands, remains of a long-drowned mountain range, rise steeply out of the deep blue of the Whitsunday Passage. Their treasures are protected by their status as a national park within a World Heritage Area.

GLORY OF THE INNER REEFS

Hill Inlet on Whitsunday Island is a safe anchorage of outstanding beauty. On the reefs close by the islands swim
bright-spotted Coral Cod, feeding on the plenty in the warm seas of the inner reefs.

CAPE TRIBULATION

On Cape Tribulation in the Daintree, the rainforest meets the reef, the thick stands of fig and palm growing to the water's edge, with just a slim crescent of beach marking the divide. Myriads of life-forms throng the rainforest, from shy Green Ringtail Possums to Cairns Birdwing Butterflies flirting with their brilliantly coloured wings.

# New South Wales and ACT

The first permanent European settlement in Australia was at Sydney Cove in Sydney Harbour. From here, colonists took convict labourers and spread up and down the coast, building the early settlements wherever they found coal, timber and farming land.

Then Blaxland, Wentworth and Lawson found a way across the Blue Mountains, and the rolling plains beyond the Great Dividing Range became fields of shimmering wheat and vast sheep stations, establishing Australia's early primary industries and fuelling legends of droving, shearing and life in the bush.

The discovery of gold in the mid-nineteenth century resulted in an influx of hopeful prospectors and opportunists from all over the world, heralding the multicultural mix that is Australia today.

Meanwhile, timber-getters cut the giant Red Cedars from the dark heart of the primordial forest of the Big Scrub, hauling the massive logs to jetties on jinkers pulled by bullock teams.

Then, in 1901, the colonies became a nation. In 1911, Canberra, from the Aboriginal word "Canberry", meaning "a meeting place", was established by Act of Parliament as Australia's seat of Federal government. The Australian Capital Territory (ACT) is surrounded by a number of national parks and reserves within New South Wales, but it was not until 1984 that the territory's first national park was proclaimed. Namadgi National Park covers more than half of the ACT, and is an untamed and complex beauty resplendent in eucalypt forests, snow gum woodlands and subalpine grasslands.

Equally glorious, New South Wales has the most varied mountain scenery and habitats in Australia. The State boasts four World Heritage Areas: the Central Eastern Rainforest Reserves; Lord Howe Island Group; the Greater Blue Mountains Area; and the Willandra Lakes Region. Other wonders include Bald Rock, New England Tableland, Warrumbungle Ranges, Jervis Bay, the Snowy River area, the Illawarra Escarpment, the High Country and the wetlands and rivers.

THE BLUE MOUNTAINS

Ferns and bracken nestle at the base of tall, straight Blue Gums that grow ever higher to trap the light that reaches into the valleys. At the Three Sisters, stunted eucalypts dig their roots into cracks in the golden sandstone cliffs and outcrops, eventually to split the rock and plunge with it to the valley floor.

GOLDEN SANDSTONES AND GREEN VALLEYS

In time, all things change. Even the soft, whispering water of Wentworth Falls cuts the rock away, grain by grain, year by year. But in these mountain valleys trees older than time have found a haven, long hidden from human eyes, and watered by a thousand streams and springs.

BOODEREE NATIONAL PARK

Craggy headlands push out into water of deepest, purest blue at Booderee, a "bay of plenty", where the proud
sea-eagle wheels above St Georges Head, and the clans gathered, from the days of their earliest forebears, to
feast on the bounty of the sea.

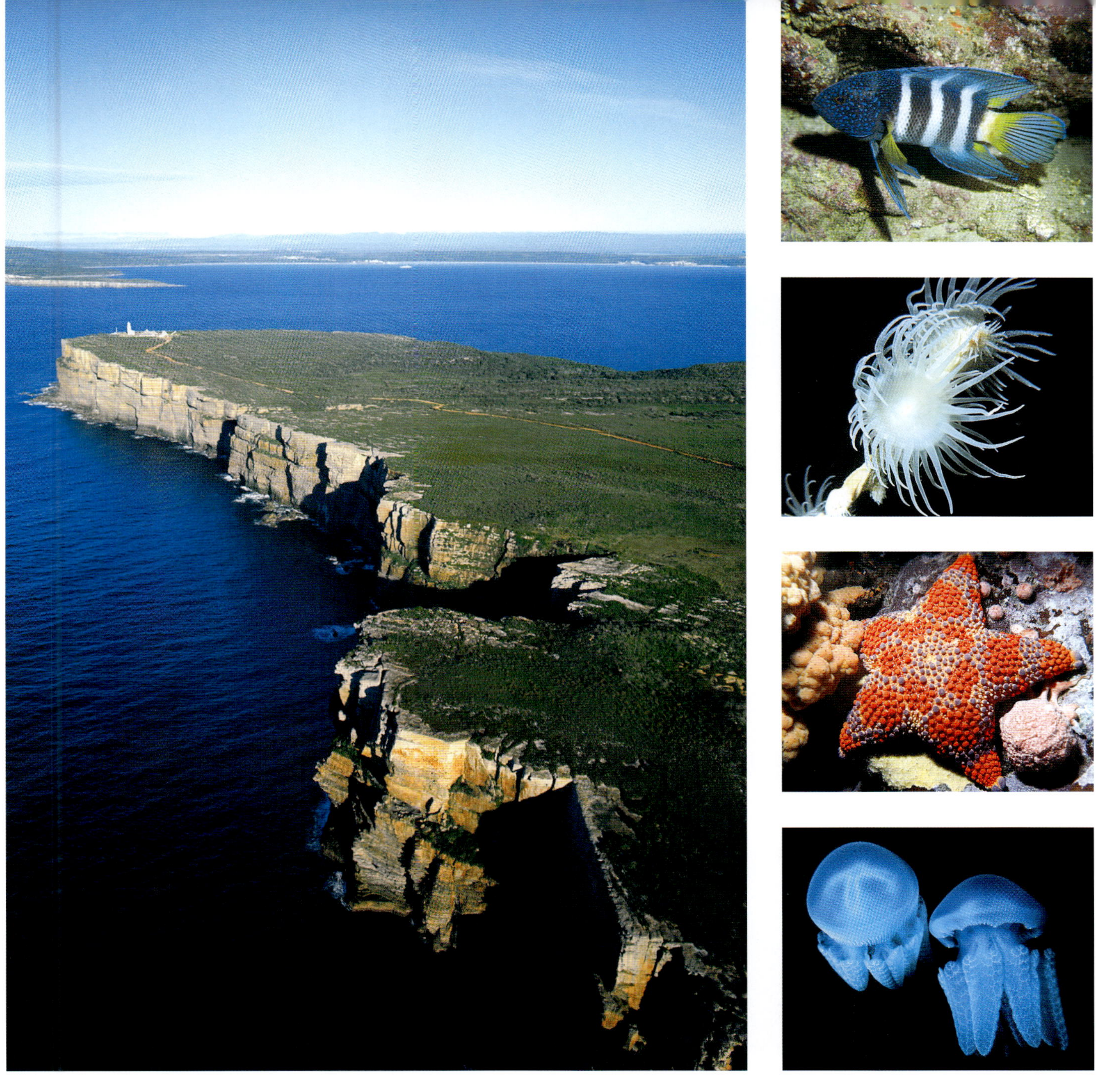

JERVIS BAY MARINE PARK

Now a lighthouse stands above the jagged stone of Point Perpendicular, like a watcher over the silent depths, where fish of every shade swim above the flaunting colours of starfish and sponges, and anemones' questing tentacles reach into the current, while jellies drift by, silent and luminous.

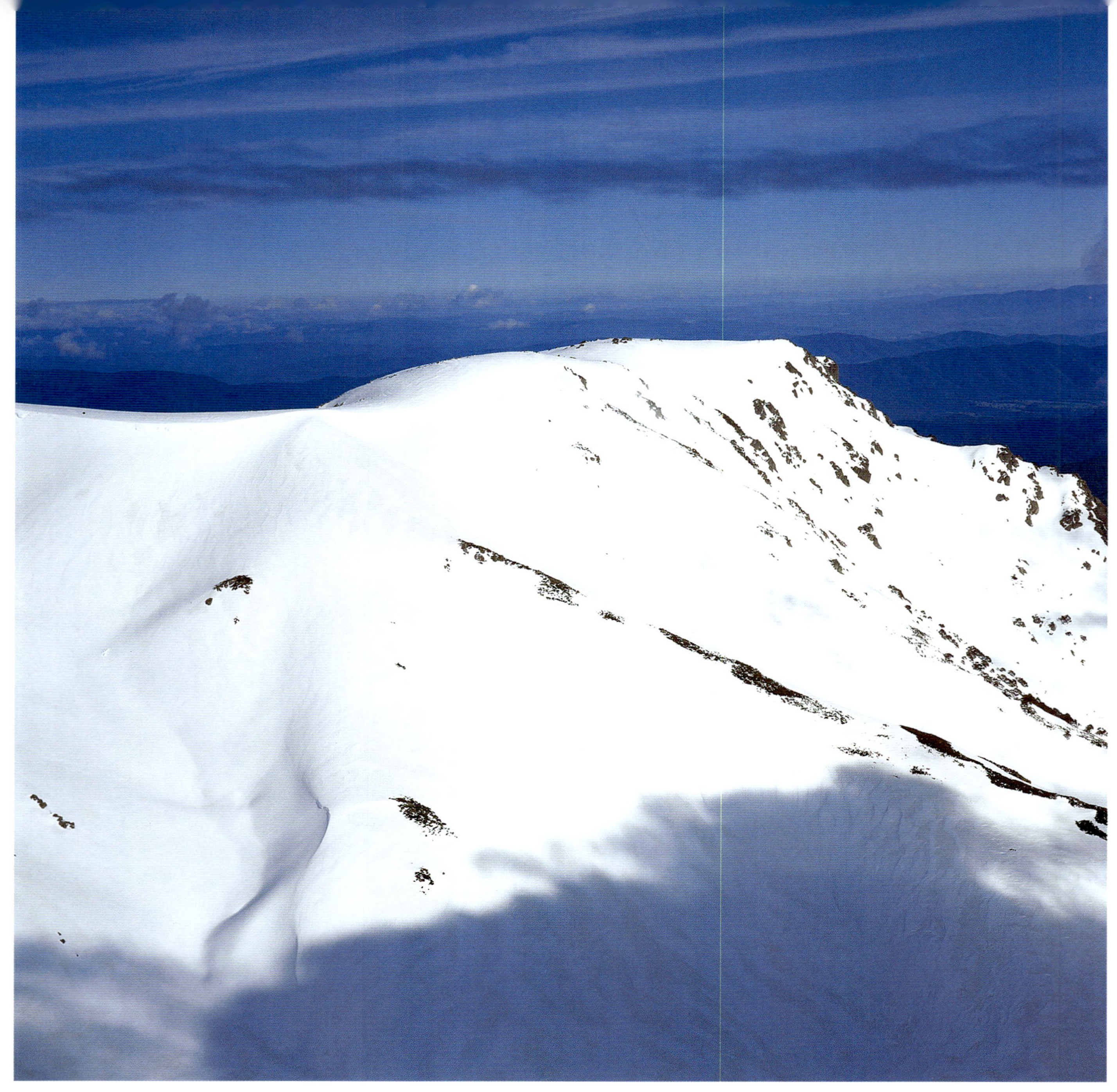

Sparkling in the sun, snow glistens white, cloaking rocky outcrops from the peaks downward; winter drapes the mountains in crystal beauty and harsh light. In spring and summer the high country sighs with gentler winds that stir flowers and lush grasses, the hard gloss of winter but a memory.

THE ROOF OF AUSTRALIA

The twisted, ravaged branches of Snow Gums sport flashes of colour, bright against the brown and white of winter. In the melt, water trickles through alpine grasses, falling into gutters between tussocks, tumbling into creeks, rushing into streams, then rivers, feeding, renewing the land.

LORD HOWE ISLAND

Volcanoes thrust up from the sea bed millennia ago now stand serenely in the turquoise ocean, sheltering birds
and plants far from other shores. Here species have changed subtly, making an island paradise unlike any other,
in their own time, and free from the cares of humankind.

NORFOLK ISLAND

Towering pines cling to steeply sloping shores battered by rolling Pacific waves that cut small bays like scalloped edging round all the coast. Harder rock stands firm… for now… and cliffs drop into the swirling sea where platforms and reefs reach out to deeper water.

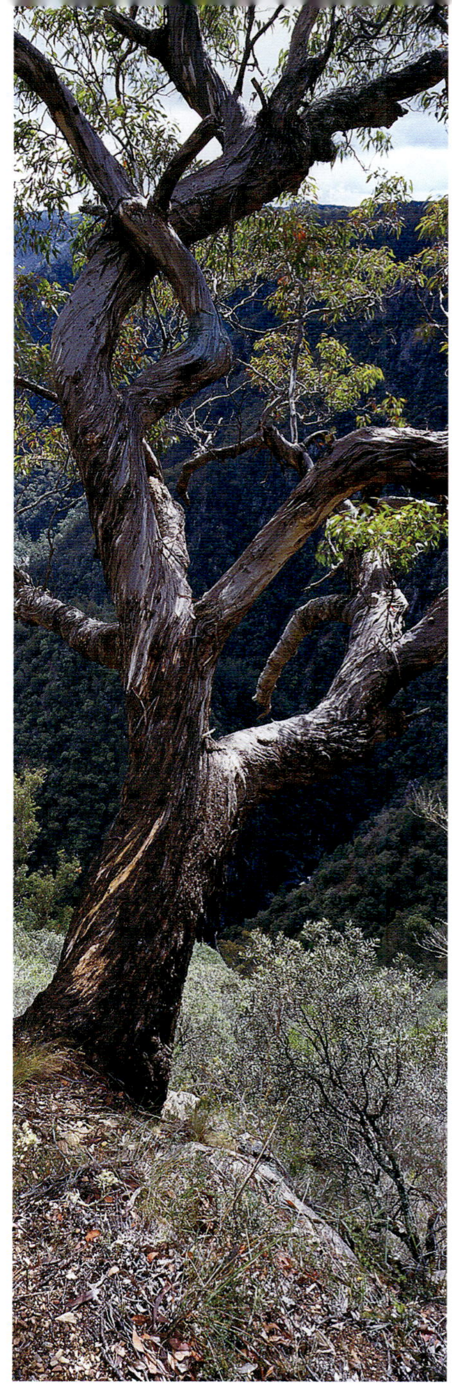

THE NEW ENGLAND TABLELAND

Great plains and eucalypt woodlands clothe the top of the tablelands, with granite boulders breaking the earth's surface. Then the land falls away, dropping swiftly to the coastal plain. The waters of Apsley Falls tumble down the basalt. Crystal Shower Falls (opposite) at Dorrigo National Park look out to the deep, fecund rainforest.

THE WARRUMBUNGLES

These "crooked mountains" loved by walkers rise from the plains, forests of wattle and gum growing close around sharp rock where the lava flows forced their way upward aeons ago. Now wild creatures flourish on this island of bush in a sea of rich grazing land and farms.

THE SOUTHERN HIGHLANDS

Clouds, riding high to clear the ranges, cool and drop rain in plenty, for it to gather in wetlands edged with sedges. From there the rising water cuts tracks outward and downward, until, sparkling and clear, Tianjara Falls plunge over the massive sandstone ramparts into gorges where verdant rainforest grows.

The ancient layers of rock stand proud, guarding the cool green depths of the narrow coastal plain, which drinks all it can from rivers and creeks fed by the many waterfalls including (left to right) Belmore, Carrington and Fitzroy Falls. All then flow out to sea, harbouring myriad life-forms where fresh water meets salt.

Victoria

Victoria, the smallest mainland State in Australia, is renowned for the natural beauty of its coast, forests, pastures and the mallee country, where the Malleefowl, resplendent in its dappled brown and cream plumage, builds huge mounds to incubate its eggs. The thick wet eucalypt forests and temperate rainforests of Mountain Ash and Myrtle Beech harbour some of the country's rare and endangered smaller marsupials, such as Leadbeater's Possum and the Long-footed Bettong. The forests of Gippsland are the haunt of the magnificent male Superb Lyrebird, where he dances and shows off his plumage on one of his display mounds, while he sings his choruses of amazing mimicry.

John Batman, a Currency Lad, sailed from Launceston into Port Phillip Bay in 1835. He settled on the spot where Melbourne has grown. It was already a thriving township when the colony of Victoria was proclaimed in July 1851 – and the discovery of gold was announced that same month. People swarmed to the goldfields from California, Great Britain, China… all the world wanted a chance to make its fortune on the rich fields of Ballarat and Bendigo. The tent cities were filled to the brim with gold-seekers, fighting, drinking, working, playing, stealing, killing, making fortunes and spending them in a day. Hard on their heels came the bushrangers, the Wild Colonial Boys of song and legend, at war with authority, particularly when it wore the uniform of an English trooper. The romance, violence and revolution of the goldfields are exciting parts of colonial history, and the riches from gold helped to build beautiful towns and cities, whose cores still stand.

The Murray River, which forms part of the border with New South Wales, is the lifeblood of the north. Paddlewheelers used it for transport; and it provides water, recreation and beauty in its sweep from its birth in the alps past huge River Red Gums on its journey west to South Australia.

Haze and gentle sea spray hang over the water, softening cliffs and stacks of glorious golden hue. On this wonderful coast the mood can change in a moment. The Twelve Apostles bear witness to the power and fury that the Southern Ocean can hurl at earth and rock, carving, shaping, ever changing the shore.

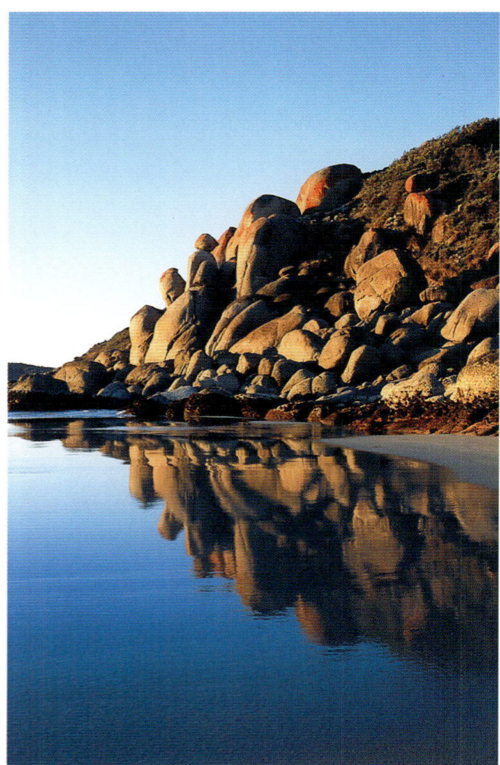

WILSONS PROMONTORY

At the southernmost point of the Australian mainland lies a spot of surpassing beauty. Among the granite tors grow rare orchids, sheltering beneath windswept bushes and among coastal heath. The sea surrounds it, reflects it, sets it off with contrasting blue, and protects it from all but one landward approach.

THE OTWAY RANGES

The misty waters of Erskine Falls, Melba Gully Creek and Hopetoun Falls (opposite) plunge into soft green depths where the ferns grow, some as big as trees, some as small as a violet. Fungi of many colours flourish in the moist air, sprouting, like strange flowers, on logs, great tree trunks and from the leaf litter of the forest floor.

PORT CAMPBELL NATIONAL PARK
Majestic cliffs guard the south-west coast against the great Southern Ocean storms and swells. But the ocean will not be denied: it cuts and carves the rock, battering it one day, gently caressing it the next.

THE GRAMPIANS

Sandstone ranges lie side by side, north to south, at the southern end of the Great Dividing Range. From vantage points, such as the Balconies (above), among the spectacular, rugged peaks and cliffs, there are views to forest and heath below where the Smooth Darling Pea blooms among the richness of Grampians flora.

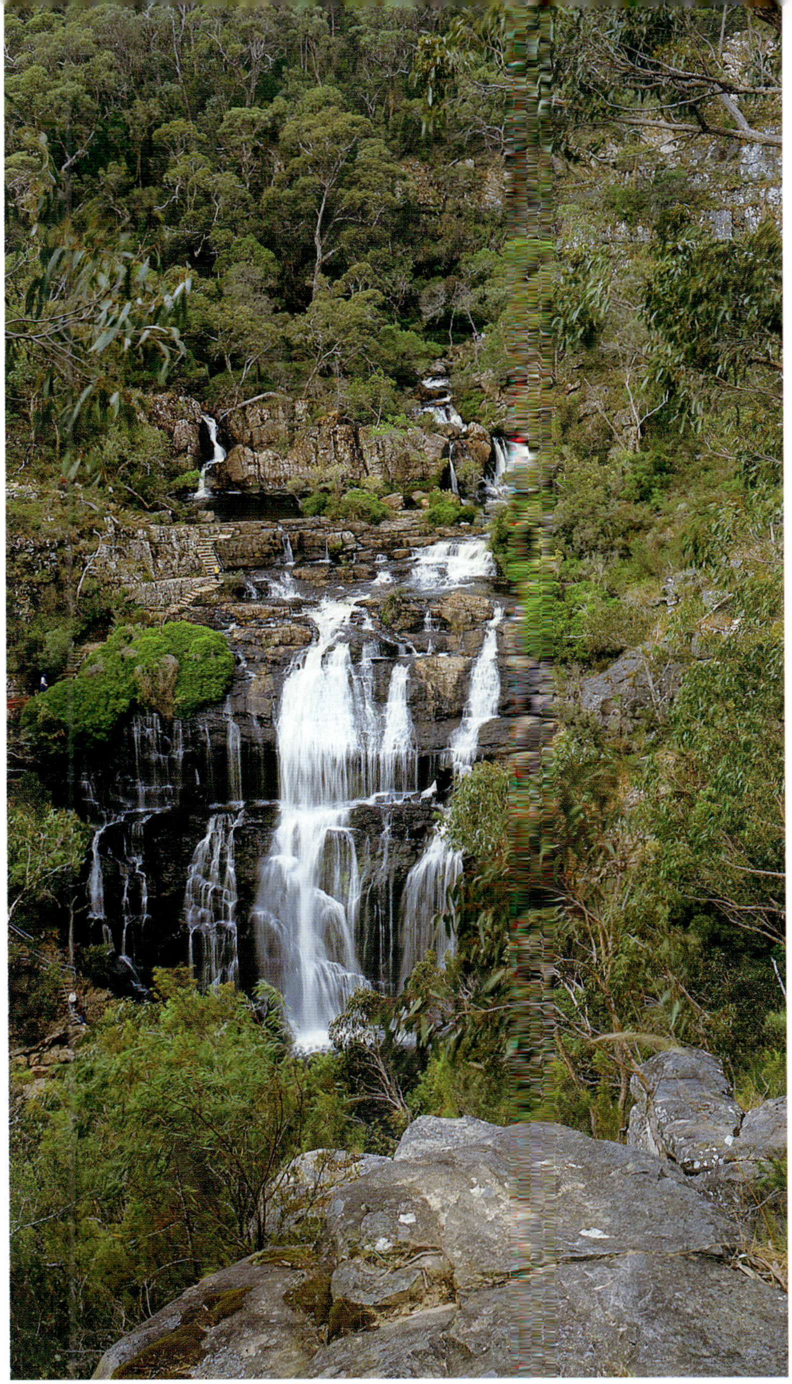

CROWN OF WESTERN VICTORIA

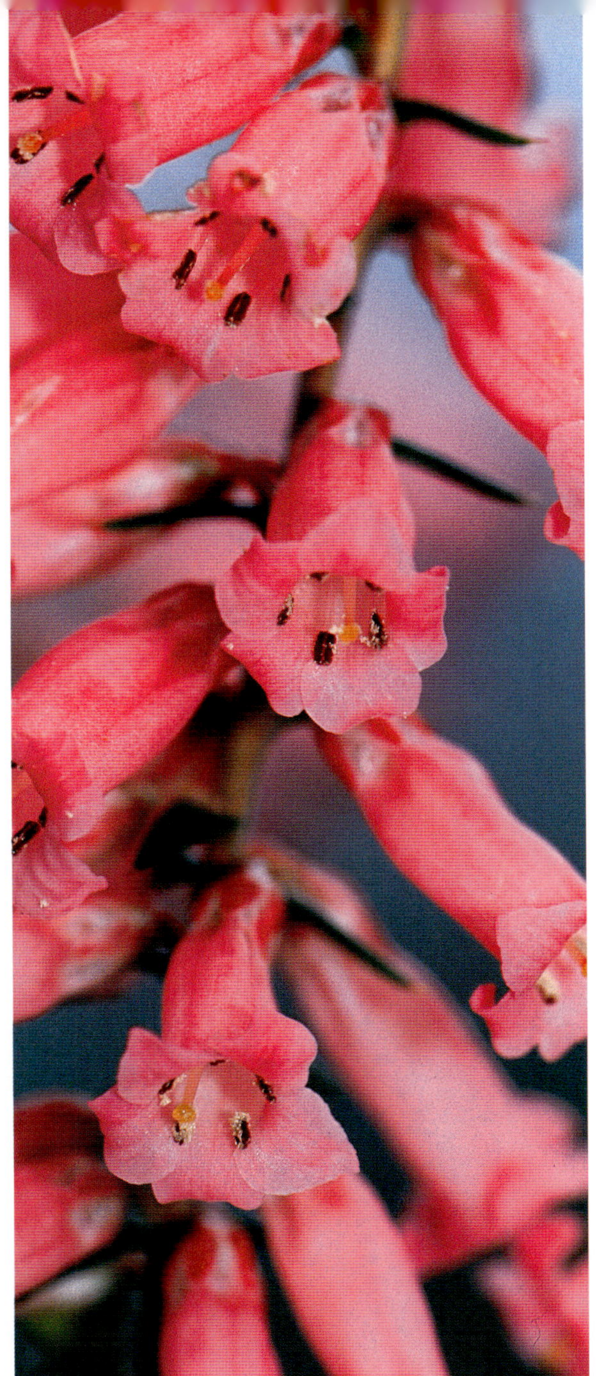

Waterfalls, like Mackenzie Falls, tumble down cliff faces, making the valleys lush and vibrantly green. On the ridges grow gums, stunted and wind-sculpted at the summits, straight and strong further down the slopes. Among them all, Common Heath and other brilliant wildflowers grow.

Tasmania

Tasmania has been an island for the last ten thousand years, ever since an Ice Age finished and the rising sea level covered the land bridge that had joined Tasmania to the mainland. And, since that time, this wonderful State has been influenced by water: the waters of Bass Strait that have kept its animals and plants safe from the likes of Dingos and Foxes; the waters of the Southern Ocean that keep its temperate climate cool and pleasant, and lash its western shores with storms, cutting off sea passage to that coast from all but the most intrepid; that same ocean, which brings seals, penguins and large seabirds to Tasmanian shores; the soft rain that falls in the cooler months, rejuvenating forests, scrub, pasture and heath; the springs on the mountains, feeding into fast-running rivers; the lakes and tarns, both natural and artificial; the water from these, used to generate power; the waterfalls and soaks, bringing rain and melt-water down to lower ground, and thence to the sea the vast river valleys, first cut by glaciers, that form harbours and havens on the coast; the passages and channels that protect boating; the marshes and the lagoons where migrating waders come to feed… all this water grants and governs life in Tasmania.

When the first European settlers came in 1803, they found a place that was, in parts, less alien than the rest of Australia. The climate was closer to that of England and the country was more amenable to farming methods that they knew. And so the convict heritage began, while free settlers built farms and small towns. But on the west coast and in the mountains the newcomers found a wilderness beyond anything they had imagined. The very density of the forests was so daunting that many have remained largely untouched, and are now protected as national parks and World Heritage wilderness.

The presence of such vast tracts of mountain country, bush and scrub, filled as it is with plants and animals now extinct or threatened on the mainland, defines Tasmania as a very special place, a place apart, a last link with Gondwana.

In the valleys and gorges, cataracts and cascades of water and spray create places where rainforest can grow.
Thick ferns frame Liffey Falls, shrouding the base of giant trees, festooned with lichens and mosses.

CRADLE MOUNTAIN

In a landscape carved by glaciers, high, wild mountains loom over lakes, pools and rushing, tinkling creeks, ancient forest, fragile alpine plants and button-grass plains. Hikers marvel at the clear air and crystal waters of Cradle Mountain and Dove Lake.

This rugged, magnificent landscape fills all with awe, scoured by wind, snow and rain on the heights, and holding fragile beauty protected in the land's folds and on its slopes. Delicate flowers such as (from top) the Grass Triggerplant, Tasmanian Waratah and the Showy Parrot Pea bloom safe from human touch.

SOUTHWEST NATIONAL PARK

This was a land of myth and legend to early settlers and convicts. The thick bush, harsh mountains and wild weather cloaked it in mystery – its very inaccessibility stirred the blood of explorers and fired the imagination of men who wanted to break free of the chain gangs.

LAND OF DEEP WILDERNESS

This same inaccessibility also fostered a haven for many animals and flora. The Short-beaked Echidna and Tasmanian Devil (opposite), Scarlet Robin and Eastern Grey Kangaroo (above) are safe in Tasmanian wilderness areas, places that nurture the Tasmanian Blue Gum (opposite) and the Tasmanian Christmas Bell (above).

Clean, pristine seas protected from the turbulence of the western winds and currents are home to the Biscuit Sea Star, the Big-bellied Sea Horse and myriad other water creatures. Divers revel in discovering this ocean of life, where the lucky few will find themselves escorted by curious sea-lions that play hide-and-seek in the kelp.

FREYCINET PENINSULA

Great knuckles of red granite stand high above green-clad lowlands and the incredible blue waters of Wineglass and Promise Bays, guarded to the north by the dramatic peaks of the Hazards. Pure white sand beaches lie in crescents between sea and bush.

South Australia

Europeans came to South Australia in 1836, when it was founded as a colony for free settlers – it is the only Australian State to be planned and built without convict labour. This is the driest State – the only permanent river is the Murray, which reaches the sea at Encounter Bay. The south-eastern corner has good, fertile soil and a blissful Mediterranean climate, which lured many of the early German settlers to plant grapevines. The vineyards of South Australia are now world-famous for the wine crushed from their grapes.

The western coasts are starkly beautiful, from the eastern end of the Nullarbor, around Eyre Peninsula, and up Spencer Gulf. This area is home to specialised wildlife, such as the Southern Hairy-nosed Wombat, which digs its labyrinthine burrows beneath the semi-arid land. In these intricate tunnel systems, the air is moister, and the wombats can spend their days in coolness and comfort, venturing out at night to eat the most succulent green shoots that they can find.

Much of the desert appears to be empty of life, but many of the animals, like the wombats, hide from the heat in burrows and in rock crevices, coming out to find food in the cool, clear nights. And then comes the time when rain teems down in western Queensland and New South Wales, Western Australia, and the flat north of South Australia itself. The run-off trickles down wandering channels, flooding out over the plains, but always, inexorably, creeping down the imperceptible drops in altitude until an inland sea of water comes to rest in the great salt lakes: Lake Eyre, Lake Torrens, Lake Gairdner.

Then follows a time of plenty for all life. Seemingly overnight plants flower in riots of colour and set seed against dry times ahead. Parrots, finches and honeyeaters breed in great numbers, as do mammals, frogs, reptiles and insects. The lakes teem with brine shrimp, which attract waterbirds to feed and nest. Gradually, the water dries up, and the Flinders Ranges again brood over orange and purple earth dotted with saltbush and spinifex.

Majestic River Red Gums grow where the water runs in times of rain, and where the moisture still seeps beneath the ground in times of drought. In all the rest of this dry, spare splendour, the Flinders Ranges rise proudly, while scrubby bush clings to life on the foothills and plains.

KANGAROO ISLAND

The beaches host sunbaking sea-lions at rest between hunting forays into the cold of the Southern Ocean. The extraordinary formations of Remarkable Rocks and the rocky shores of Kangaroo Island never fail to fascinate.

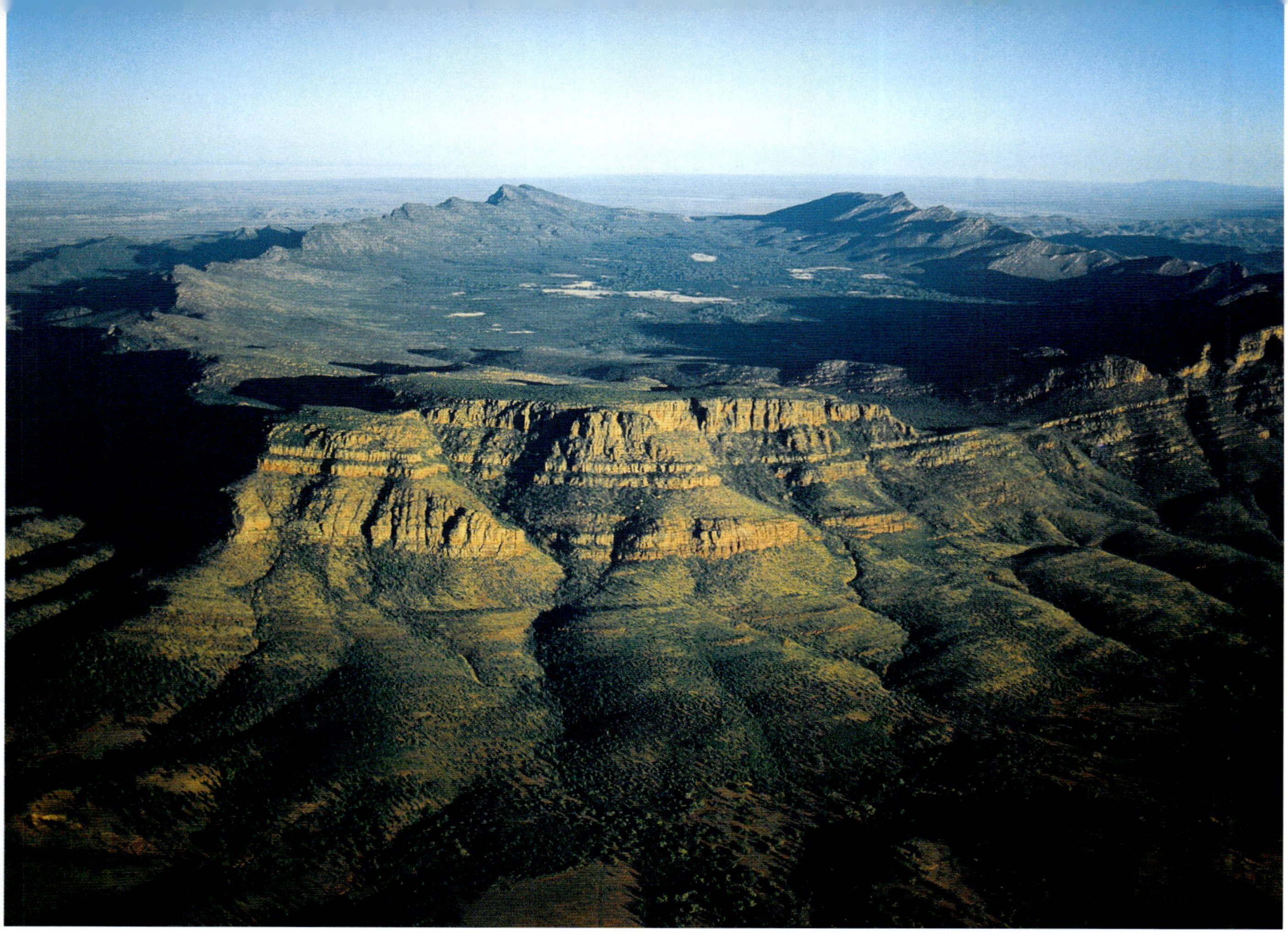

THE FLINDERS RANGES

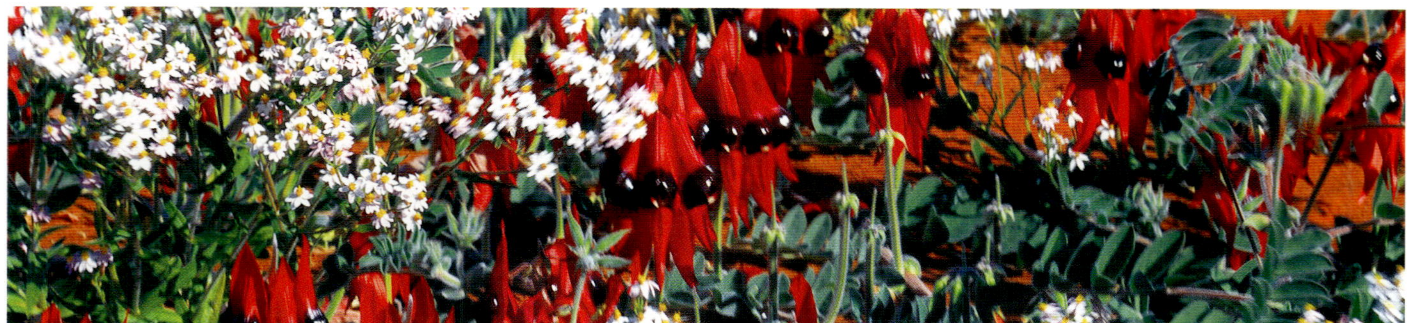

Wilpena Pound, a natural amphitheatre, is ringed by mountains that plunge steep to the plain, a natural haven where grass and trees flourish in the harsh Outback. In springtime, the vibrant red of Sturt's Desert Pea stands out among the wildflowers. Throughout the dry ranges, creekbeds are lined with venerable River Red Gums.

COFFIN BAY NATIONAL PARK

This is a place of extremes – great beauty, and harshness; gentle waters, and wild, rolling surf; long, barren lines of wind-blown dunes, and thickets of tea-tree; sweeping, softly shelving beaches, and sheer, gaunt cliffs. Above it all wheel the White-bellied Sea-Eagle and the Osprey, while the Australian Pelicans rest below.

Western Australia

The majority of Australians live on the eastern seaboard, and are used to looking east to the water and cooling breezes, but the citizens of Western Australia, the vast wonderland that is Australia's biggest state by far, have the opposite view – the Fremantle Doctor eases in from the west on hot summer afternoons, cooling Perth, the capital, built on the banks of the Swan River.

Albany and Perth were the first two European towns in the west; both were established by the late 1820s. For a long time the population stayed in the fertile, well-watered south-west corner, gradually moving out into the grain-belt developed beyond the coast. Slowly the east and the north of the great State were explored by the newcomers as prospectors hunted for gold and the cattle kings drove their mobs across inland Queensland, the Gulf and the Top End to the Kimberley.

It seems that the geology and mineral wealth of Western Australia is made to a giant's scale to match the land itself: there are mountains of iron in the Pilbara; the Argyle Diamond Mine is the largest in the world; and more gold has come out of the Kalgoorlie field than any other in Australia – and it is still being mined. But the land has great and savage beauty that has nothing to do with its mineral wealth; it is a majestic and awe-inspiring place of immense distances, and of an ancient culture based in the Dreaming, the very beginnings of life as told in Aboriginal Australia. The land holds evidence of its great age – in Hamelin Pool at Shark Bay can be found stromatolites, the "living rocks" that have survived for about 2000 million years.

The plants of the west are distinctive and many are unique – the wildflowers there grow with an abundance and variety unknown in the east, and their colours range over a palette of complexity and delicacy, while the Karri and the Tingle, the giant trees of the south-west, are found nowhere else. Many shy mammals have found their last haven here, saved by distance from the ravages of incoming predators. This is the great western land.

Strange, rounded, dome-like hills of white sandstone stained red with iron, all tiger-striped with lichen, the Bungle Bungles in Purnululu National Park crowd together, a symbol of Australia's mystery, and the unknown heart of this great land: they were unknown to any but the Aboriginal people until the 1980s.

THE GREAT SOUTH-WEST
Coasts of incredible variety and heathland bursting with flowers fringe the south-west corner.
Clockwise from top left: wildflowers; Fitzgerald River National Park; Two Peoples Bay; Elephant Rocks, William Bay
National Park; Flinders River National Park; Salmon Holes, Torndirrup National Park. Opposite: Sugarloaf Rock,
Leeuwin–Naturaliste National Park.

STIRLING RANGE NATIONAL PARK

A chain of mountain peaks are etched against the sky, with gentle foothills and heath wrapping around them.
The hills and heath are clothed in glory each spring, when such fanciful flowers as (from top) Pink Fairy, Queen
of Sheba and Dianella Lily bloom in all the hues of an artist's yearning.

WALPOLE–NORNALUP NATIONAL PARK

Full seventy-five metres into the air soar the topmost branches of the mighty Red Tingles and Karri. Their timbers are much sought-after, and their conservation and management are issues that concern governments and community groups. These forest giants are unique to this south-west corner, and bring thousands to marvel.

NAMBUNG NATIONAL PARK

Strange and unearthly, the Pinnacles rise from a desert of sand. The southerly winds blow, alternately burying and
unearthing these limestone columns as the millennia pass by.

KALBARRI NATIONAL PARK
Aeons ago, multicoloured masses of Tumblegooda Sandstone was thrust up from beneath the sea. The elements then carved and moulded the stone to create Nature's Window (above left). The Murchison River has cut through the rock, and made the land bloom with (from top) Southern Cross, Albany Daisies, and Pink Riceflowers.

SHARK BAY MARINE PARK

Richly coloured sand, shaded from gold through to deep red, lies in drifts across the Peron Peninsula, right to the edge of Zuytdorp Cliffs (opposite, bottom). Water of deepest, purest blue laps the shore, and beneath the water are seagrass meadows where the peaceful Dugong grazes.

KARIJINI NATIONAL PARK

Summer's heat shimmers in the air, so dense that it seems impossible to breathe. Water is more precious than gold in this land where creeks and rivers barely nurture the scant trees, bushes and grass that scratch out life on the hot earth and rocks, glowing red from a rich base of iron oxide.

THE HAMERSLEY RANGE

But the water is held in deep pools in the valleys at the base of waterfalls such as Joffre Falls (opposite) and Fortescue Falls (above). In spring, bursts of birdsong herald the start of each day. Then the flowers are blooming, and the air is like honey, and life spins its circle as it ever has done.

THE KIMBERLEY

In the north-west lies a plateau forgotten by time where the scratchy arms of boabs are etched against the sky,
and the records of the first people of this land adorn rocky walls.

A LAND OF ADVENTURE

Clockwise from top left: Bell Creek Gorge, King Leopold National Park; the Bungle Bungle Range, Purnululu National Park; Fitzroy River, Geikie Gorge National Park; Lennard River, Windjana Gorge National Park.

Northern Territory

The Territory has the vibrancy and panache of a frontier settlement. Battered by war and nature, the citizens know that nothing is unchanging; that the past is always with us, powerful and enduring, but that the surface of life can change in a breath.

Darwin is a new city, being settled in the 1860s and rebuilt in the 1970s, and it is closer to Asia and New Guinea than to any other Australian capital. This makes the people outward-looking, and, even though they value their status as Territorians, they come from many backgrounds and traditions, which they also keep alive and vibrant. Darwin is the definition of multi-culturalism.

The Territory's two halves contrast bewitchingly. In the south lie the deserts, the burning red lands that glow in the sun's light. Rocks, sand, dry riverbeds, stunted trees and spinifex bake in the heat, springing to life when the rare rains fall. Then the ephemeral plants spring up, flowering in a riot of colour, and every living thing, from the greatest to the smallest, rushes to create a new generation before the dry regains its hold. But in the desert are valleys and gorges where permanent water can be found, and in them echoes remain of a wetter world that has gone. Their lushness emphasises the sere majesty of the desert, which supports a surprisingly heavy burden of life.

In the north are the wetlands, flooding out to the horizon in the wet, shrinking back in the dry. Masses of lilies dance on the floodplains, while flocks of birds darken the sky. Above the plain are the ramparts of stone, the escarpment. First come the wild thunderstorms, firing tinder-dry grasses, then Ubirr, the stone country, catches the clouds and harvests the monsoon. Great volumes of water tumble down from the plateau to the plain, waterfalls roaring, filling the air with thunderous voices, gushing down canyons, racing out to the sea. Crocodiles bask in the sun, while the richness of life fills every heart with hope.

Uluru – one mighty rock is the nation's heart. Also known as Ayers Rock, it stands proud above the desert, a monument to the past and present of this oldest, most fragile, and yet hardy land.

ULU<u>R</u>U–KATA T<u>J</u>U<u>T</u>A NATIONAL PARK

Like dreams from prehistory, Ulu<u>r</u>u (above) and Kata T<u>j</u>u<u>t</u>a (once known as the Olgas, opposite) loom over the
plains, visible for an eternity in the clear desert air. They catch the sunset, burning red as a fire, after changing
hue all day with each variation in the light. These are the heart of belief and spirit for their custodians.

THE MACDONNELL RANGES

Layered, folded, thrust upward, weathered, covered by the sea, then uncovered again, the mountains still stand high above the plain. Mighty Wedge-tailed Eagles soar on the thermal currents above them, while Black-footed Rock-wallabies (above) and wallaroos (opposite) shelter in gullies and leap, rock to rock.

AND WEST MACDONNELL NATIONAL PARK

The Arrernte people have had custodianship of this country since time began. It is an ancient landscape that has been shaped by nature for thousands of years. Its grandeur and timeless beauty encompass exposed peaks and ridges and secret gorges where permanent water sustains plant and animal life.

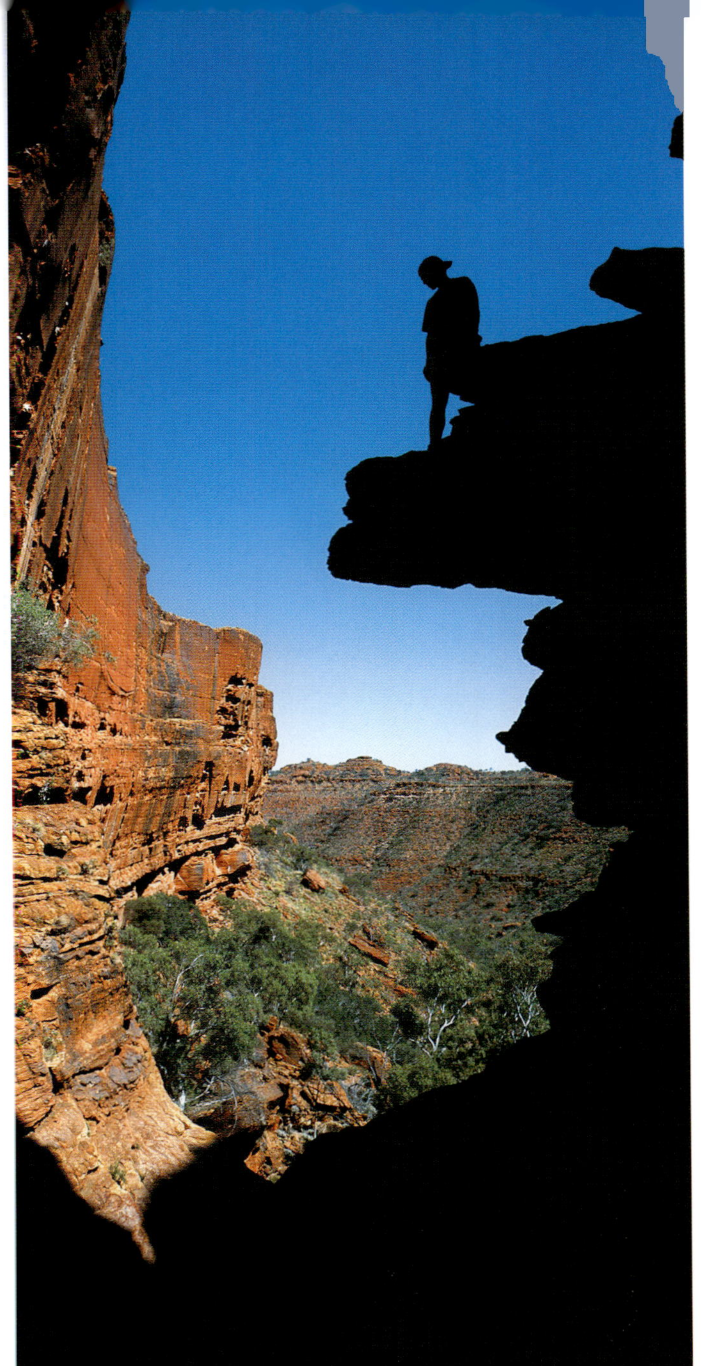

WATARRKA NATIONAL PARK

Sheer walls of fractured sandstone encompass a deep ravine where water filters down through the porous rock to lie, shaded and cool, and make an oasis of life. Remnant plants are protected by the overshadowing cliffs of Kings Canyon, clinging to existence, waiting for the climate to change.

LITCHFIELD NATIONAL PARK

In the north, at the top of a sandstone plateau covered in dry woodland and forest, springs feed into creeks that cut channels leading to lower ground. Wangi Falls (above) and Florence Falls (opposite) cascade down chutes in the stone, buffeting and leaping in cataracts, filling deep pools in rainforest hidden below.

KAKADU NATIONAL PARK

Anbangbang Billabong and the floodplains throng with waterbirds: elegant Jabirus tread the shallows with measured gait, while ducks and geese paddle and waddle, the Jacana treads lightly, long toes spanning the lily pads, while stilts skitter through the shallows, one eye looking for danger below, one eye on the sky.

THE NEVER NEVER

Plains and dry woodland go on for ever, green and fresh after the monsoons, bone coloured in the dry. Mobs of cattle graze this expansive country, country cut by weathered gorges and marked by the strange, sculpted rock formations of the Lost City in the Tawallah Range, a land of eerie magic, and spirits and tales of the Dreaming.

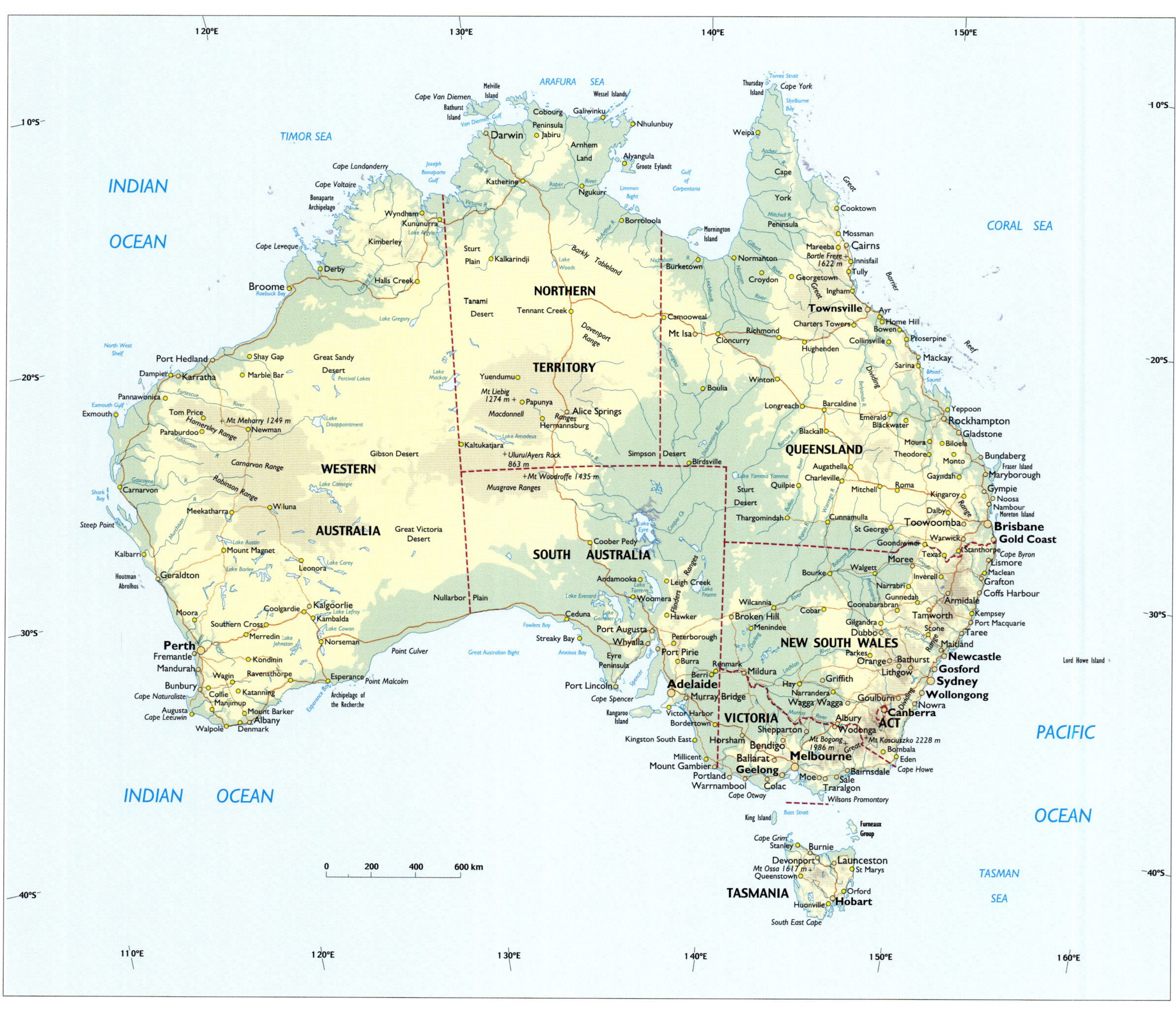

INDIAN OCEAN
TIMOR SEA
ARAFURA SEA
CORAL SEA
PACIFIC OCEAN
TASMAN SEA
Great Australian Bight

NORTHERN TERRITORY
WESTERN AUSTRALIA
SOUTH AUSTRALIA
QUEENSLAND
NEW SOUTH WALES
VICTORIA
TASMANIA
ACT

Darwin
Jabiru
Katherine
Ngukurr
Borroloola
Wyndham
Kununurra
Kimberley
Derby
Halls Creek
Broome
Port Hedland
Dampier
Karratha
Marble Bar
Shay Gap
Pannawonica
Exmouth
Tom Price
Paraburdoo
Newman
Mt Meharry 1249 m
Hamersley Range
Carnarvon
Meekatharra
Wiluna
Mount Magnet
Leonora
Kalbarri
Geraldton
Moora
Southern Cross
Merredin
Coolgardie
Kalgoorlie
Kambalda
Norseman
Perth
Fremantle
Mandurah
Wagin
Kondinin
Ravensthorpe
Esperance
Bunbury
Collie
Katanning
Manjimup
Mount Barker
Albany
Denmark
Walpole
Augusta
Cape Leeuwin

Kalkarindji
Tennant Creek
Tanami Desert
Great Sandy Desert
Gibson Desert
Great Victoria Desert
Yuendumu
Mt Liebig 1274 m
Papunya
Alice Springs
Hermannsburg
Macdonnell Ranges
Kaltukatjara
Uluru/Ayers Rock 863 m
Mt Woodroffe 1435 m
Musgrave Ranges
Coober Pedy
Nullarbor Plain
Ceduna
Streaky Bay
Andamooka
Leigh Creek
Woomera
Hawker
Port Augusta
Whyalla
Port Pirie
Port Lincoln
Peterborough
Burra
Adelaide
Murray Bridge
Victor Harbor
Kingston South East
Bordertown

Camooweal
Burketown
Normanton
Croydon
Georgetown
Mt Isa
Cloncurry
Richmond
Hughenden
Winton
Longreach
Barcaldine
Blackall
Boulia
Birdsville
Simpson Desert
Sturt Desert
Thargomindah
Quilpie
Charleville
Augathella
Mitchell
Cunnamulla
St George
Goondiwindi
Thursday Island
Cape York
Weipa
Cooktown
Mossman
Mareeba
Cairns
Innisfail
Tully
Ingham
Townsville
Ayr
Home Hill
Bowen
Proserpine
Charters Towers
Collinsville
Mackay
Sarina
Emerald
Blackwater
Yeppoon
Rockhampton
Gladstone
Moura
Biloela
Theodore
Monto
Bundaberg
Maryborough
Gympie
Noosa
Nambour
Dalby
Toowoomba
Brisbane
Gold Coast
Warwick
Stanthorpe
Texas
Moree
Inverell
Narrabri
Grafton
Coffs Harbour
Armidale
Tamworth
Gunnedah
Coonabarabran
Gilgandra
Dubbo
Kempsey
Port Macquarie
Taree
Scone
Maitland
Newcastle
Gosford
Sydney
Wollongong
Bourke
Cobar
Wilcannia
Broken Hill
Menindee
Parkes
Orange
Bathurst
Lithgow
Canberra
Goulburn
Nowra
Griffith
Hay
Narrandera
Wagga Wagga
Albury
Wodonga
Mildura
Renmark
Berri
Horsham
Bendigo
Ballarat
Geelong
Melbourne
Shepparton
Mt Bogong 1986 m
Mt Kosciuszko 2228 m
Bombala
Eden
Cape Howe
Moe
Sale
Bairnsdale
Traralgon
Wilsons Promontory
Millicent
Mount Gambier
Portland
Warrnambool
Colac
Cape Otway

King Island
Cape Grim
Stanley
Burnie
Devonport
Mt Ossa 1617 m
Queenstown
Launceston
St Marys
Huonville
Hobart
Orford
South East Cape
Furneaux Group

0 200 400 600 km

Index of photographs

From an early age, Steve Parish has been driven by his undying passion for Australia to photograph every aspect of its wild places. Then he began to turn his camera on Australians, the places they live in, and their ways of life. This body of work forms one of Australia's most diverse photographic libraries. Over the years, his images have been used in thousands of publications from cards, calendars and stationery to books – pictorial, reference, guide and children's. Steve has combined his considerable talents as a photographer, writer, poet and public speaker with his acute sense of needs in the marketplace to create a publishing company that today is recognised world wide.

Steve's primary goal is to share Australia with the world. This book is one of a collection designed to do just that. Take a visual journey through Steve Parish's Australia. See its grace, sense its charm, all join in the fun.

We invite you to visit the Steve Parish Publishing websites where you can view Steve's wide range of products and participate in Australia's only photographic travel e-zine.

online

FOR PRODUCTS
www.steveparish.com.au

View books, calendars, diaries, children's books, stationery and gifts.

FOR LIMITED EDITION PRINTS
www.steveparishexhibits.com.au

View a selection of wildlife, wildflower and landscape photographs with options for framing and purchase.

FOR PHOTOGRAPHY EZINE
www.photographaustralia.com.au

Join discussions on photographing Australia, photo tips, photo locations, competitions, freebies and more.

Photography: Steve Parish
Text: Wynne Webber
Design: Elise Crooks

Front cover: Uluṟu, Uluṟu–Kata Tjuṯa National Park, Australia

Map by MAPgraphics Pty Ltd, Australia

Printed in Hong Kong by South China Printing Co. Ltd

Film by Colour Chiefs Digital Imaging, Australia

Produced in Australia at the Steve Parish Publishing Studios